# What's It Like to Be President?

by Dick Morris

Illustrations by Clayton Liotta

Designed by HOOKMEDIA Design Studio

ISBN: 978-0-615-82619-6

# Table of Contents

# Introduction

Dick Morris knows what it is like to be president. During his two years at the White House (from 1995-1996), he was the chief advisor to President Bill Clinton. So heavily did the president rely on Morris' advice that one jealous aide was moved to write: "for nine months, Dick Morris really *was* President of the United States."

With our children exposed to a barrage of news about the government, they may not understand what they are seeing and hearing. Since public schools regularly cut out Social Studies classes for budgetary reasons and slant the teaching they do on the subject to make it politically correct, we need to fill this enormous void. The voters of tomorrow are not getting the education they need to cast informed ballots.

Dick's book gives them the background they need and cannot get elsewhere. He does so in easy-to-read text augmented by cute color cartoons and informative sidebars. He tells the exciting story of the passage of the welfare reform bill in 1995-1996 to show how the government process works. This narrative is fast paced, engrossing, and accurate.

Dick was my political advisor in Arkansas when I was first elected to statewide office in 1992. I loved working with him and since then we have cultivated a deep and enduring relationship. Behind the scenes, he was very helpful to me when I was running for president in 2008.

He showed wit and spirit and great good humor...and also extraordinary patience.

If I learned that Dick was my son's Social Studies teacher, I would be thrilled. Now, we have the next best thing – his understanding and profound insights in a book that fifth graders and above will love and enjoy. And the cartoons are neat!

Dick's book tells young people what goes on in Washington, how it works, and why its important. Because I know and love Dick Morris, I can enthusiastically recommend this work to the entire home school community.


## Mike Huckabee

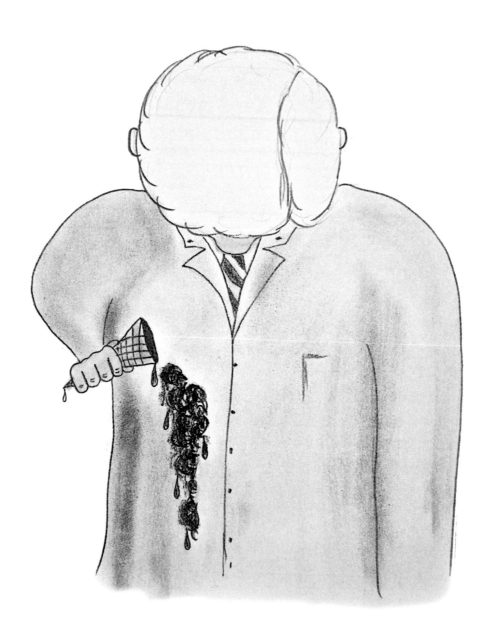

# Chapter One:
## The President is Calling

President Bill Clinton was in trouble. And he knew it. Elected in 1992, defeating President George H.W. Bush (father of our recent president George W. Bush), he had been swept into office with strong Democratic majorities in both the House of Representatives and the Senate.

"And now," he thought to himself, "I've blown it."

A Democrat himself, Clinton knew that he had had an opportunity few new presidents ever have – the members of his own party had majorities in the two houses that made up the U.S. Congress. Now he could persuade Congress to pass his ideas and make them laws.

In our system of government, we have a president who is elected directly

## How Is Congress Set Up?

In our Constitution, the president and the Congress are two equal parts of the government. They are independent. In many countries, they are elected together and the Congress appoints the president (usually called the Prime Minister). But in the U.S. they are elected separately.

The members of the House of Representatives are each elected from their own district. Their districts are usually fairly small, with fewer than one million people in each one. They have to run every two years, so they are directly influenced by public opinion.

The president is elected by the country as a whole. We all vote on who should be president. He has to run for office every four years.

There are two senators from each state, so their districts are much bigger than those of Congressmen. They only run every six years, so they are a lot less effected by public opinion.

Each part of the government is different and influenced by different forces. They are often in conflict. We call that system "checks and balances." Nobody has total power.

by the voters and serves for four years. He can run for a second four year term, but no more after that. And then there is Congress – which is equal to the president in power. Congress has two Houses: The Senate and the House of Representatives. There are 100 Senators, two from each state and 435 Congressmen. The whole country is divided up into districts and each Congressman represents one of them.

## Who Are Your State's Two Senators?
## And Who is Your Congressman?

For a law to be passed, a majority (more than half) of the Senators and Congressmen must vote yes and the president must sign the bill. If the president does not sign the bill, he vetoes it which means he disagrees with it. If a president vetoes a bill, it is not a law unless two out of every three Senators and Congressman vote to pass it again. If they do, they are said to "override" his veto and the bill becomes law.

So when President Clinton found out that he had been elected president in 1992 and that more Democrats than Republicans were elected to the House of Representatives and the Senate, he thought it meant that he could pass all the bills he wanted to.

But it hadn't worked out that way. Not exactly. Clinton was able to pass some of his programs, but not the ones he valued most – health care reform and welfare reform. It is true that more than half the members of

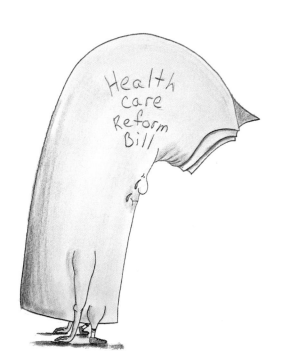

Congress were from his own party, but some of them disagreed with President Clinton on each of these important bills and voted against them even though they were Democrats. The Republicans almost always disagreed and, together, the Republicans and a few of the Democrats were enough to defeat the bill.

Then, to make things even worse, in the elections of 1994, just two years after his own election, Clinton's Democrats lost control of both houses of Congress.

Under the constitution, every two years there is an election for Congress. In that election, every single member of the House of Representatives has to run again to be able to return to Congress for a new term. Senators are luckier. They serve for six years, so every year one out of every three Senators has to run again.

Why did the people who wrote the constitution set it up that way? They wanted the people to control the government, so they provided that the House of Representatives would be elected directly by the people every two years – all of them. But they also thought that maybe sometimes people would think they wanted something and would vote that way only to realize in the future that they had made a mistake. So the men who wrote the Constitution provided that they could change their minds. While every member of the House of Representatives was elected every two years, only one out of every three Senators was elected every two years. So it took six years – three elections – for the Senate to change completely. That way, they reasoned, one house – the House of Representatives – would follow closely what the voters wanted, but the other House – the Senate – could stop and think about a new idea and maybe make the country wait a little bit before adopting it. Because each Senator served for six years, he could worry less about each change in the mood of the people and think more about the longer term.

So in 1992, the Democrats won majorities in both houses of Congress. But, in 1994, the Republicans came back and threw the Democrats out. Now, the party opposed to Clinton – the Republicans – would take over. No longer would he be able to assume that he would get the support of the Congress. More likely, he would face their criticism at every turn.

That was when he called me. "Dick, I'm in trouble," he said as soon as I came to the phone. "I need you here."

I'm Dick Morris. I was Bill Clinton's chief advisor when he was governor of Arkansas, before he was elected president. But I had not followed him to Washington. Actually, after I had worked for Clinton for fifteen years, I had become more of a Republican than a Democrat, so, except for some phone calls with the president and his wife, the First Lady Hillary Clinton, from time to time, I stayed pretty much away from the White House. Clinton and

## Chapter One: The President is Calling

I liked each other still, but we were not working together closely like we did in Arkansas.

But now, it was different. My old friend was in trouble and he asked me to come down to Washington to help out.

When the president calls you and you pick up the phone, the first thing you hear is a person saying your name: "Mr. Morris? The president wants to speak with you." You find yourself wondering, "president of what?" My local bank? The Parent Teacher Association? The Rotary Club? No, the President of the United States!

The Secret Service, charged with guarding him, calls him POTUS – the initials of President of the United States.

A lot of times, he places the call but he's not ready to talk. He's finishing up another call. So you wait. And you wait. And you wait. "What's he calling about?" Your mind races. "Is he mad? Did I mess up? What's happening? Is there something I missed in the newspaper this morning?"

Finally, he came on the phone. "I've lost my majorities in both houses and I'm in tough shape," he began. "I need you to come down here and rescue me. Like you did last time," he added with a chuckle.

"Last time" had been back in 1981. And now it was November of 1994. Clinton was first elected Governor of Arkansas in 1978, at the age of 32. But when he wanted a second term, in 1980, he lost. I had worked for him in 1978 but he fired me after that and I was not there for his campaign in

1980 – the one he lost. But after his defeat, he welcomed me back. Hillary called and asked me to come to Arkansas. I went there and helped Clinton get elected again the next time up – in 1982. Now things were playing out the same way.

We both knew that in 1996, President Clinton's four year term would be over and, to get another term, he would have to ask the voters to make him president again (re-elect him). And the voters weren't in the mood to do that right then. My job was to help to change their minds and get Clinton re-elected.

*Should the whole Congress be elected every two years or should it be like it is now when the House of Representatives is elected every two years but only one-third of the Senate is elected every two years?*

*Some say: It should stay as it is because we need to make sure that people are not swept away with an idea or a popular person but that there are others who can sit back and take a more long term view.*

*Others say: It should change. We are a democracy. That means government by the people. If we want to change the way our government is working, we should be able to change all of it every two years without having to wait for six years to do so.*

# Chapter Two:
## President Clinton Has a Good Idea

Throughout that year, 1995, President Clinton and I worked very hard to improve his image with the American people. Newspapers poll every week or so to measure a president's popularity. And President Clinton was moving up. But not fast enough.

Right after Christmas in 1995, when the White House ushers were taking down the Christmas tree that tens of thousands of people line up to see each year, he asked me to come to the White House office for a talk.

Actually, it wasn't his office. It was his home. The president lives and works in the White House. To keep things straight, there is a West Wing where he keeps his office and an East Wing where he and his family live.

The West Wing is crowded with people, each pressing for a few minutes

of the president's time.  And crowded, too, with reporters anxious to see who is entering and leaving the president's office.  The West Wing office is shaped like an Oval.  It has bright colors – yellow and blue – and looks like nobody ever messes it up.

The East Wing is another story. That's where the president's family – including his daughter Chelsea, who was 15 then – all lived.  It was in the Treaty Room of the East Wing, his elegant home office on the second floor, that I always met the president.  It was in that room that William McKinley signed the treaty that ended the Spanish-American War in 1898.  It was a beautiful room with extremely high ceilings and windows.  It was painted a burgundy red. The floor was covered with a huge Persian rug colored in teal and burgundy. A large leather couch was on one side of the room across from a chair and ottoman in a stripe reflecting the colors in the room.  It had the warm feel of a comfortable club library.

But there is something that reminds you that this is not just a comfortable club library. Sitting outside the room, on a chair right by the door, was a soldier – usually a Marine – holding a hard leather briefcase – an attaché case – on his lap. He always travelled with the president and when President Clinton was in the room, he was right there sitting outside with his case.

I knew what was in the case. It contained the machine through which the president could order our nuclear missiles to attack any country that was attacking us. The President wore a key chain around his neck. The key, in this machine, would launch the missiles. Some people felt that such an attack might mean the end of the world. We all knew that it would kill many, many millions of people.

It was pretty awesome to see that soldier each time I met the president.

But war was not on the president's mind as he walked in the door. "We've got to press new ideas," he began. He knew that he would not be re-elected unless he became more popular with the American people. His low poll numbers were bothering him. And me.

The president remembered how he had campaigned on the slogan that he would "end welfare as we know it." Now, he said, "lets keep the promise."

End welfare? Wow! That was a tall order. Welfare was the program that gave people who didn't have jobs money so they could eat and pay the rent. It was for mothers who had children but didn't have any husband to help pay the bills. Almost twelve million people depended on it. Nobody wanted to end welfare. But the president did want to curb the abuses.

And there were abuses! In many families, the mothers had always been on welfare. And their mothers. And their mother's mothers. Generation after generation not working, having babies, never having a father to help with the bills, and waiting for the government to send a welfare check.

## What Is A Sound Bite?

A "sound bite" is a short phrase that politicians use to explain complicated subjects. They do it because very often the news on television will not let them take enough time to explain their opinions in depth, so they use the "sound bite" to communicate what they want to say.

People who had to get up each morning and go to work were sick and tired of paying the welfare costs. They said, "why should I go to work everyday and pay taxes so my tax money can go to somebody who can work but doesn't?"

Those who defended welfare disagreed. They said that almost all the people on welfare were single mothers – unmarried women who had a child, often several children, to raise. The defenders of welfare said that these mothers needed to care for their children during the day so they couldn't work.

But the people who criticized welfare did not see things that way. They pointed out that tens of millions of mothers worked and raised children, leaving them with relatives or in a day care center or a school while they were at work. "Why couldn't these women do the same?" they asked. In fact, they said that the welfare program itself offered to pay for day care for the mother's children if she wanted to work. "The fact is that these mothers do not want to work," these critics of welfare said.

Some even accused welfare mothers of just having babies because they got more welfare with each new baby.

People who defended welfare pointed out that the benefits were pretty low and that it probably cost more to have another child than you would get in extra payments.

# What Do Liberals and Conservatives Think?
# Where Do They Disagree?

In politics, some people are liberals and some are conservatives. Then, there are people who are in-between and they are called moderates. Most Democrats are liberals and most Republicans are conservative.

**Liberals generally believe in:**

- ✓ More government spending
- ✓ Higher taxes, particularly for wealthy people
- ✓ More welfare for the poor
- ✓ That people shouldn't be allowed to have guns
- ✓ That government must pass lots of rules to make sure businesses and people are doing the right thing
- ✓ That we should not punish people who commit crimes too harshly
- ✓ That abortion is OK
- ✓ That men should be allowed to marry other men and women to marry other women
- ✓ That religion and moral values should not be taught in school

**Conservatives generally believe:**

- ✓ In less government spending and lower taxes
- ✓ In fewer rules for businesses and people to have to follow
- ✓ That criminals should be punished severely
- ✓ That welfare should be reduced
- ✓ That people should be allowed to own guns
- ✓ That abortion is wrong and should not be allowed
- ✓ That marriage should only be between a woman and a man
- ✓ That children should be taught moral and religious values in school

Let's imagine that Mr. Liberal and Ms. Conservative were having a debate. It might go something like this:

**Mr. Liberal:** There are too many poor people who don't have enough to eat or good housing to live in. Let's increase government spending and give them more money.

**Ms. Conservative:** I agree that there are a lot of needy people, but where would the government get the money to help them out? It would come from taxes and taxes are the money we collect from people who get up each morning and go to work. Why should we take from them and give to the others?

**Mr. Liberal:** Oh, I don't want to take money from ordinary people, just from rich people who can afford it.

**Ms. Conservative:** Wait a minute! Who hires the ordinary people to work for them? Who creates a job that they can have? Not poor people. Not even what you call ordinary people. No, they don't have the money.  Rich people do.  So when you take money from rich peo-ple, they cannot afford to pay ordinary people to work for them.  And then the ordinary people cannot afford to pay taxes to help the poor.

**Mr. Liberal**: But we are a very rich country.  Can't we afford to help people?

**Ms. Conservative**:  But we do already.  We pay old people Social Security and pay for their medical care through Medicare.  We pro-vide free schools for children and pay for their medical care, too.  We help any poor person who cannot make enough money to pay for himself.  That is what welfare and Medicaid are for.  But if we give away too much money, we won't have enough left to create real jobs so people don't become poor.  The more we give money to the poor, the more poor we create!

**Mr. Liberal**: How can we expect single mothers to work?

**Ms. Conservative**: I know lots of single moms who work very hard.  They leave their children with Grandma or in day care.  Millions of single moms work.  Why can't they work instead of going on welfare?

And so on.  Liberals and conservatives see things very differently.

The situation was getting worse.  More and more money was being spent on welfare.  Something had to change.

When he was campaigning, Bill Clinton said, "Welfare is OK in times of need, but not as a way of life.  It should be a helping hand, not a hand out."

A "helping hand, not a hand out." That was a neat way to say it.  In pol-itics, that is called a "sound bite."

Even though the sound bite was easy to say, it was hard to accomplish the changes.

In fact, both liberals and conservatives disagreed with him!

Liberals wanted welfare to continue just as it was. They were afraid that if it were cut, then poor people wouldn't have enough to eat or a place to live. They said "don't cut funds for needy children and their mothers!"

The conservatives wanted to cut welfare so it only went to those who really needed it. They said "don't waste our tax money on people who don't want to work!"

But President Clinton had a better idea, a mixture of the liberal and the conservative ideas.

He said: "Keep giving people welfare, but make them work for the money. No more just sitting around. If they can't find jobs, the government will give them jobs – sweeping streets, cleaning museums, doing odd jobs. If they don't work, they don't get welfare."

"And," he said, "limit how long people can stay on welfare. Pass time limits. Five years maximum. That's it. After that, government has done all it can to help them, and then they are on their own."

Of course, everybody agreed that people who couldn't work because of serious disabilities would not have to. They could still get benefits. But all people who physically could work would have to.

Clinton said that people on welfare were "stuck." He said, "They're trapped there. They'd like to get out but they don't think they can."

"So give them jobs, job training for better jobs, and a time limit to get off welfare." That was Clinton's idea.

**Think about it...**

*Would you say that you are more of a conservative or a liberal? Why? In what ways are you more conservative? In what ways are you more liberal?*

# Chapter Three:
## The Republicans Have Their Own Idea

Usually, when a president thinks up an idea, he has his staff write up a bill doing what he proposes. (A bill is a law that hasn't been passed yet.) He then persuades one or more members of the Senate and some from the House of Representatives to introduce the bill in Congress. When they introduce a bill, they give it to the clerk and ask the Senate or the House to consider it. Then, the clerk assigns the bill to a committee to study it.

But, in this case, there already was a bill about reforming welfare that had been introduced into both the House of Representatives and the Senate. It was a bill sponsored by Republicans, members of the party that opposed President Clinton – and they controlled a majority of each house.

## Chapter Three: The Republicans Have Their Own Idea

The Republican bill did what the president wanted and required people to work in order to get welfare. However, it also cut a lot of programs Bill Clinton thought people really needed that should not be cut.

For example, the people on welfare generally did not own cars and many couldn't even afford to take buses every day. So how were they going to get to the new jobs the president wanted them to take? Most lived too far to walk to work. How would they get there? The president wanted to help them pay for their bus fare. But the Republican bill didn't do that.

And what would the single mothers do with their children while they were at work? Some could leave them with grandparents, but many couldn't. So President Clinton wanted the government to pay for day care where the children could go during the day when their mothers worked. The Republicans didn't like the idea.

And Clinton was worried that many people would get jobs that didn't pay very well and that they would find that they made more money from welfare than from their new jobs. In that case, it wouldn't take a genius to figure out that they would do better not working and staying at home.

So President Clinton said we should give them more government aid if they did work than if they didn't. He wanted to give the poor people who left welfare to take new jobs extra food stamps (stamps that you can give the checkout person at the supermarket and get food for free) and he wanted to send each of them extra money above the amount they made at their jobs, but only if they were actually working. Those that didn't work wouldn't get the extra check.

But the Republicans objected saying "if you spend all this money on these new programs, you won't be saving the taxpayers any money."

"Not at first," the president answered, "but once these women on welfare get used to working and get better and better jobs, we can cut back on

this extra aid and they can pay for their own day care and transportation like we all do, but not at first."

The Republicans debated with President Clinton, usually speaking through their two leaders in Congress, one in the House of Representatives and one in the Senate.

In the House, the leader of the majority party is called the "Speaker." That doesn't mean he talks a lot. It means that he runs the House of Representatives. He is elected by a majority of the members. So if there are more Republicans than Democrats in the House, as there were in 1995, the Speaker is Republican. His name was Newt Gingrich, a Congressman from Georgia. You've probably seen him on television. He has white, white hair – and a lot of it!

The Senate is also run by someone elected by a majority of the members. But he is not called the "Speaker." He is called the "Majority Leader." His name in 1995 was Bob Dole. He was the Senator from Kansas.

So, between them, Newt Gingrich and Bob Dole – both Republicans – ran the Congress.

They wouldn't listen to President Clinton's objections to their welfare reform bill so they brought it to the floor without making any changes. "Bringing a bill to the floor" means that you ask the committee that is studying the bill to make a report urging Congress to approve the bill or not and ask each member of Congress to vote yes or no on the bill.

The Republican bill did part of what the president wanted. It required people on welfare to take jobs and limited the time they could be on welfare. But it left out all of the extra benefits President Clinton wanted to give them to help them work and to make sure that working paid them more than welfare did.

The Republican bill cut out money for transportation and day care. "How are they going to get to work?" President Clinton asked. "Who will care for their children when they are at work?" The Republican bill had no answers. And it also cut out the extra food stamps and the checks people that worked would get from the government to be sure that working gave them more money than welfare did.

Generally, when the majority party in Congress supports a bill, it gets enough votes to pass easily. Most of the Senators and Congressmen from one party think a lot like the others who are members of their party and will vote the way the rest of them do.

And so it was with the welfare reform bill. The Senate and the House of Representatives both passed the bill with all the Republicans and a few of the Democrats voting yes and the rest voting no. The Constitution provided that when a majority – more than half – of the members of each House voted yes, the bill was approved. When both Houses approved the bill, it went to the White House for President Clinton to approve or disapprove.

**Think about it...**

*Do you think it was better to spend extra money on transportation, day care for children, and extra pay and food stamps for people on welfare as long as they took jobs and worked?*

*Some say: Yes! Otherwise how could the welfare mothers get to work and care for their children?*

*Others say: No! It is a waste of money. They can always get a ride from someone and leave their children with family. After all, they don't stay home all day now. They go out shopping and for other things, so why can't they get their own transportation and day care like they do now?*

or

# Chapter Four:
## President Clinton Faces a Tough Decision

From the moment the Republican welfare bill landed on President Clinton's desk, he had a very tough decision about whether or not to sign it.

A lot of President Clinton's advisors wanted him to veto the bill. George Stephanopoulos, one of his main advisers, was more liberal than I was. George said he should veto it because it left out all the important programs President Clinton had included.

"Why shouldn't he sign it?" I challenged George. "It does what we want. It makes welfare mothers work and sets a time limit on their ability to stay on welfare."

"Yes," he conceded, "but it also cuts transportation payments, day care, and everything else."

## How A President OKs A Bill

If a president agrees with a bill, he signs his name to the bottom and that makes it become a law. Everyone has to obey the law so his decision is very important.

But sometimes a president disagrees with a bill and does not want it to become a law. In that case, the Constitution says he can "veto" a bill. He vetoes a bill by refusing to sign at the bottom and tells the Congress what he doesn't like about it and why he is vetoing it. Sometimes the president can even veto a bill by refusing to sign or veto it. He just doesn't do anything and the bill never becomes a law. That is called a pocket veto. He just puts the bill in his pocket and forgets about it.

Of course, once the president vetoes a bill that isn't the final word. The constitution says that the bill then goes back to Congress where the House and the Senate can override his veto – approve the bill and make it into a law even though the president has vetoed it. To do that, two out of every three Senators and Congressmen have to vote to approve the law despite the veto.

In the U.S., the president cannot veto part of a bill. He either has to approve (sign) the whole thing or kill it entirely. So the Republicans thought that the cuts would lead Clinton to veto the whole bill.

But that is very hard to do and President Clinton knew that while the Republicans could get a majority vote (one half plus one) in each house of Congress, they couldn't get two-thirds (two out of three votes).

One of the reasons the decision on whether to sign or veto this welfare reform bill was so tough had to do with President Clinton's political history.

He was the first Democrat to be elected president in sixteen years. The

Democrats had lost three presidential elections in a row – in 1980, 1984, and 1988. Most people thought they would lose in 1992 also. They lost all these years because people thought that their candidates were too liberal. That meant that they wanted to spend too much government money, raise taxes too much, not do enough to punish criminals, and continue to let people stay on welfare without working.

But President Clinton said that he was a "different kind of Democrat." He said he was a "new Democrat." By that he meant that he would not go along with the things the past Democrats had favored. For example, he favored very tough penalties against people who commit crimes. He said he did not want to raise taxes. And, most of all, he said that he wanted to "end welfare as we know it."

When voters heard Bill Clinton say he wanted to "end welfare as we know it," that sounded pretty good to them. It meant that he was not like the Democratic liberals who didn't mind just handing out checks to people month after month without asking them to work or anything.

But after President Clinton was elected in 1992 and he took office in

1993 (a president is elected in November and takes office in January, two and a half months later), he did not do what he said he would do before the election.

He said he would not increase taxes, but he did.

He had said that he would cut government spending, but he didn't.

And he said he would "end welfare as we know it" but he didn't.

So a lot of voters felt that President Clinton had not been telling them the truth when he ran for president and voted against his candidates in the 1994 elections. That's why the Republicans took over the House and the Senate. And that's why President Clinton had asked me to come down to Washington to help him to get re-elected.

President Clinton had been making a real effort to persuade people that he was a moderate, not a liberal.

Moderates are not liberals or conservatives. They are in between. They agree with a lot of what liberals think and also with a lot of what conservatives think. They are a little liberal and a little conservative at the same time. Both parties try to compete to win the votes of moderates because neither liberals nor conservatives on their own give them enough votes to win elections. It is only by adding in the moderates that they can hope to win.

I felt that Clinton needed to stop being a liberal and be more of a moderate. And I felt that the best way to show this change would be to pass welfare reform. If he vetoed the bill, I said that it would mean that he was never a moderate at all, but was a liberal all along. I told him that he could not win an election that way.

The Republicans knew this, of course, and they wanted to show that President Clinton was still a liberal and not a moderate. They passed the welfare reform bill partly because they really believed in it, but also because they felt that if President Clinton vetoed the bill, they could say "see, he is not a moderate after all. He is still too liberal." And maybe they could defeat him in 1996.

"That's why the Republicans made these cuts in day care and transportation and put them in the bill," the president said. "The goal of the Republicans is not to reform welfare, but to force me to veto a welfare reform bill so they can say I didn't mean it when I said in the campaign that I'd end welfare as we know it. So they cut all these other programs to force me to veto it."

"Now they will run around the country saying 'President Clinton promised to reform welfare but when we passed a bill that did what he suggested, he vetoed it. You can't trust President Clinton.'"

Some of the loudest voices urging him to veto the Republican bill came from the Department of Health and Human Services (HHS). The president doesn't do his job alone. He has fifteen or twenty agencies to help him. These agencies – called Departments – have been set up over the

# The President's Cabinet

George Washington himself set up the first four Departments: The State Department to work on relations with other countries, the Treasury Department to pay the government's bills, the Attorney General who heads the Justice Department to be the government's lawyer, and the War Department to supervise the country's military. That was his whole Cabinet.

Over the two hundred twenty-four years since then, a lot of new Departments have been added. **Here is the list of the entire Cabinet today:**

- Secretary of State
- Secretary of Treasury
- Secretary of Defense
- Attorney General
- Secretary of the Interior
- Secretary of Commerce
- Secretary of Labor
- Secretary of Health and Human Services
- Secretary of Housing and Urban Development
- Secretary of Transportation
- Secretary of Energy
- Secretary of Education
- Secretary of Veterans Affairs
- Secretary of Homeland Security

And then there are some Departments that are not in the Cabinet but their heads are considered to be of "Cabinet rank."

- Environmental Protection Administration
- US Trade Representatives
- Ambassador to the United Nations
- Office of Management and Budget
- Council of Economic Advisors
- Small Business Administration

years by different presidents and each one is headed by a "Secretary." Originally there were only four Departments and four Secretaries.

Over the years, many other Departments have been added as the work of the president has grown. While the Constitution does not say anything about these Departments, all presidents have agreed that they need them to do their work.

The heads of each Department – called Secretaries – meet together every few weeks with the president. They are called the president's "cabinet."

The head of the Department of Health and Human Services was an old friend of mine, Donna Shalala. (pronounced shah-lay-la). She believed very strongly in helping poor people as did the many thousands of men and women who worked for her in the Department. She was generally against making people on welfare work or setting time limits for how long they could stay on welfare. But she knew that President Clinton supported these ideas, so she went along with him even though they disagreed in private.

Why would the liberals, the Democrats and the people under Donna Shalala oppose making welfare mothers work in order to get benefits? Why were they against limiting the time people could spend on welfare? They said that people on welfare have the right to ask their fellow citizens to help them out. They said that these people did not choose to be poor

## The Right to Vote

Years ago, only white men with money could vote. Then, about a hundred and eighty years ago, all men were allowed to vote whether they had money or not. One hundred and fifty years ago, after the Civil War, black men — African-Americans — got the right to vote. It wasn't until one hundred years ago that women got the right to vote.

but were hurting because they were born to broken families, brought up in bad neighborhoods, educated at bad schools, and became pregnant at too young an age. They were really just children themselves having children of their own.

The liberals said that they should be able to spend time at home with their children making sure that they grew up to be more successful than they themselves had been. They said that to make them work at low paying dead end jobs did not do them any good and having them away from home would do their children real harm.

Clinton answered that the key was to get them off welfare and into good paying jobs so that they and their children could have a shot at a better life. After all, he would say, how is welfare working out for them? Their mothers were generally on welfare. And their grandmothers. And their children would probably be as well. We have to break the cycle with this generation, the president said.

So make them take jobs. Provide the jobs if they cannot find them on their own. Pay them decently. Give them free medical care (Medicaid), free day care for their children, food stamps so they could eat better, help with the bus fare to get to work and extra money when they come home so that they are not poor. But, he said, the key was to ask them to do their part – to work full time and show up for work every day.

It is not a "one way street" where government gives out money and the people that get it don't have to do anything. Clinton insisted it had to be

a two way street. "We will do our part – to get them help – but they have to do theirs, to work hard," Clinton said.

Some conservatives (people opposed to more government spending) worried that Donna Shalala and her staff were not interested in having people leave welfare at all. They said that if the people left welfare, Donna and her staff would have less power and many of *them* would lose their jobs. And they didn't want that!

A president is free to do what he wants and does not have to follow the advice of his Departments, Secretaries, or Cabinet. But President Clinton was very worried about disagreeing with Donna Shalala since he respected her opinion and advice. He also knew that poor people can each vote under our Constitution and that if Donna Shalala said President Clinton was not doing a good job of helping them that he might lose their votes. So he did not disagree with Donna if he could help it.

The media – radio, television, newspapers, and magazines – also began to express their opinions about the Republican welfare bill. Some strongly urged the president to veto it while others said he should sign it. Every day, everyone told the president what to do.

In many countries, they can't do that. But the Constitution gives everyone the right to say and think what they want. It's called Freedom of Speech and Freedom of the Press and it is guaranteed by the very first amendment to the Constitution.

## The Bill of Rights

As soon as the Constitution was written and adopted by the states, a lot of people wanted amendments limiting the power of the new government. They were worried that it would do what every other government in the world used to do – stop people from speaking their opinions if they disagreed with the government's. So the people and their representatives in Congress passed ten amendments to the Constitution saying what the government could and could not do. They are called the Bill of Rights and they guarantee that anyone can criticize the president anytime they want without fear.

**Here is the Bill of Rights:**

**First Amendment:** Guarantees freedom of speech, press, and religion. It lets people speak to Congress by sending in petitions and to meet together to discuss their opinions as long as they do it peacefully.

**Second Amendment:** The people can own guns.

**Third Amendment:** The government cannot make people share their homes with soldiers unless they want to.

**Fourth Amendment:** The government cannot search you or your home unless a judge says it is OK and there is a good reason to allow it.

**Fifth Amendment:** Nobody has to confess to any crime he may or may not have committed. You cannot try a person for a crime unless a special jury says there is a good reason to suspect that he did it. Nobody can be tried twice for the same crime. The government cannot take away your property (land, car, things you own) unless a court rules that it is OK – and then they have to pay you its value.

**Sixth Amendment:** Anyone accused of a crime has the right to a trial very soon after they are accused. He can ask to be tried by a jury of people like him. The government has to tell him what it thinks he did and to let him or his lawyer question anyone who is a witness against him. He has the right to make his own witnesses speak for him and he has the right to have a lawyer.

**Seventh Amendment:** Even when no crime is involved and people are just fighting in court over money, each side has the right to ask for a jury trial.

**Eighth Amendment:** Cruel or very harsh punishment for a crime (like whipping or torture) is illegal

**Ninth Amendment:** People have many rights that are not listed here.

**Tenth Amendment:** The government in Washington can only do the things listed in the Constitution. Anything else is left for each of the states to do.

So, in America, you can say what you think and make sure the president hears your advice. And boy did people give him advice! Every day each side pounded President Clinton with their opinions.

The liberals said that welfare was an important "safety net." By that they were drawing a comparison with a tightrope walker at the circus who walked on a rope strung high above the ground. One false step and he would fall off. But to stop him from being really hurt, the circus owners would install a net beneath him. If he fell, he would just hit the net which would break his fall and would not hit the ground which would break his neck!

The liberals were saying that if somebody fell on hard times, lost their job, or got sick, they needed a "safety net" just like the circus tightrope walker so that they would not be killed and could get back up and try again.

But, President Clinton said, welfare was becoming much more than a safety net, used only once in awhile when people fell. People weren't getting back up to try again. They were just staying in the net, doing nothing. It was more like a big soft bed with lots of pillows where people could sleep and would not have to work while other people had to work hard and pay taxes to support them. Clinton favored a safety net, but not a bed!

Finally, after listening to everybody, President Clinton decided to veto the bill.

"I agree with the need to make people on welfare work and with the need to limit the time they can be on welfare," he said when he vetoed it. But, he pointed out that this bill cuts day care, transportation, food stamps, and the extra checks people need so that their new jobs pay more than welfare did. He said that if Congress passed a new bill without these extra cuts, then he would sign it and make it a law.

Think about it...

*Do you think a welfare mother should have to leave home and go to work every day in order to get welfare benefits?*

*Some say Yes! Unless we force them to work, they will not take jobs but will just stay home and collect welfare. If we make them work, they will get used to getting up in the morning, putting on good clothes, and going to work. The more they get used to it, the better they will be at working. They will move up to new and better jobs and leave their life of poverty (poverty is another way of saying "being poor") and welfare way behind.*

*Others say No! People should be free to decide whether or not to work. Particularly mothers should have the right to choose to stay home with their children during the day. That way they can help bring them up as good citizens with good values.*

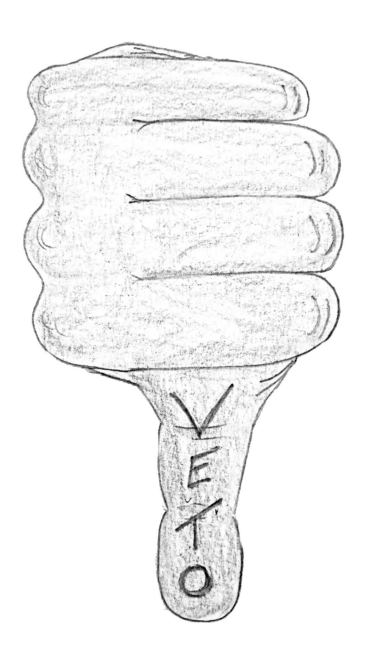

# Chapter Five:
## The Republicans Try Another Move

When they heard that President Clinton had vetoed their welfare reform bill, the Republicans went ballistic! Crazy!

"We told you he did not mean what he said about reforming welfare," Gingrich and Dole said. "He just pretended to be for it to get elected and to get people to vote for him."

Since most people supported changing the welfare system, his veto hurt his chances for re-election. But he held strongly to his views. "I couldn't sign that bill," he told me. "Not and sleep well at night."

"Don't worry," I told him. "The Republicans will pass another bill and this one maybe you'll be able to sign."

I knew what I was talking about because one of my very good friends was

the Republican Senator from Mississippi, Trent Lott. Trent was very high up in the leadership of the Republicans in the Senate. He was actually the number two Republican there. His boss, Senator Bob Dole from Kansas, was the leader of the Senate's Republicans. His title was "Majority Leader" and the head of the Democrats was "Minority Leader." If the Democrats regained the majority, they would switch titles. Dole, as Majority Leader in the Senate was the equal of Newt Gingrich who was Speaker of the House of Representatives.

But Bob Dole had something else on his mind. He wanted to be president. He was planning to run against Bill Clinton in 1996. So he wore two hats: One as Majority Leader of the Senate and the other as a candidate to run against Clinton.

Sometimes these two roles conflicted with each other. As Senator, Bob Dole may have wanted to vote for a bill, but as a presidential candidate against President Clinton, he might vote against it so that Clinton would not get the credit for the bill passing. In fact, some Republicans were getting a bit annoyed at Dole's having to play two roles at the same time.

Many of the Republicans in the Senate would have liked to have passed a welfare reform bill that President Clinton would sign. Senator Lott was one of them.  He felt that it was important to end the cycle of generations living on welfare and that requiring them to work and setting time limits was the way to go.  But, while Dole agreed in principle, he did not want Clinton to sign a welfare reform bill because he wanted to use the veto as an issue against him in the 1996 campaign, just as Clinton had suspected.

So I asked Trent Lott what he could do to change the welfare bill to make it possible for Clinton to sign it.  "We can restore some of the money for transportation so they can get to work and we can also put some of the day care money back in the bill." He also said that he might be able to trim some of the cuts in food stamps and in government aid to those who were working.  I told him that might be enough for the president to sign the bill. I reported back to Clinton.

"Sounds like a deal," he said.  "That's a bill I can sign."

But even as President Clinton was saying those words, Senator Dole was attacking him for vetoing the welfare bill.  "He says one thing and does the other," Dole said lashing out at Clinton.  "You can't trust him."

And Republicans all over the country were singing the same tune as Dole, criticizing Clinton.  They ignored the fact that Clinton was willing — even eager — to sign a bill that made people work and limited their time on welfare.  It was the other cuts in the bill that made him veto it.  But the Republicans never said that.

On the other hand, all of the officials at the Health and Human Services Department – the people who worked for Donna Shalala – were happy with the veto.  They opposed making people work for welfare or setting time limits and were glad Clinton vetoed the bill.  They, too, never mentioned that the reason for the veto was the other cuts that were included in the bill.

But President Clinton kept challenging the Republicans to pass a bill he would sign – one that required work for benefits and set time limits while it did not cut other programs.  Trent Lott promised to do his best, but he still had to contend with Senator Dole who did not want to get a bill passed. He would rather have the issue to hit Clinton with.

Welfare is only one of the programs that the federal government runs. All of these programs are listed in a document called the Federal budget. Welfare was only a fairly small part of the budget. But another program aimed at helping poor people called Medicaid was much more expensive.

Medicaid money is spent on providing health care to the poor. The idea is that they cannot afford to pay for it themselves and that they also cannot afford to buy health insurance.

(Health insurance is a way you can pay a set amount of money each month to an insurance company. That payment is called a "premium." If you are healthy, you may never need to touch the money you have paid in premiums. But if you do get sick and need a lot of care, you can use the money you have paid to the insurance company in premiums to pay for your medical care. And, you can also use the money other people have paid in their premiums that they are not going to need because they are healthy.)

Medicaid pays for older people who have to stay in nursing homes and for younger people who are too poor to pay for their own medical care.

The Republicans wanted to cut Medicaid. They felt that its costs were rising because people were seeing doctors when they didn't need to and that hospitals and doctors were charging too much money for their services.

The Republicans had a good point. Medical costs were going up very fast and most people believed that as long as the federal government was willing to pay for the doctors visits, there would be more and more of them whether they were needed or not. Everyone agreed there was a lot of waste in the Medicaid program. Sometimes doctors – who made more money the more often they saw a patient – would ask people to come back to see them when they did not need to or would send them to another doctor when it really was not necessary (and the other doctor would send his patients to the original doctor so they both could get extra money). Republicans wanted to cut the program to eliminate this waste.

But Democrats worried that important services would be cut rather than just waste. They worried that old people might not be able to stay in nursing homes even though they were too sick or too weak to care for themselves at home.

It always seems that both parties are a little bit right! The Democrats are right that we do not want to cut help to people who really need it. The Republicans are right that a lot of the money is wasted and some is even paid to people who shouldn't get it. So the question always is how to cut the waste but not hurt the really needy.

President Clinton wanted to keep the welfare and Medicaid issues separate. He knew that if he tried to cut Medicaid, he would face a lot of opposition from doctors, hospitals, and poor people. He would rather deal with welfare first and Medicaid later.

Everybody in the government and in the Congress had an opinion on welfare reform. Some were for it and others were against it. But there were also lots and lots of people outside the government who cared a lot about these issues. How could they make the government and Congress listen to their opinions?

## What is a Lobbyist?

Lobbyists are often former members of Congress who have retired or people who have spent their lives following Congress and seeing how it works. The lobbyists charge their clients (the people who hire them) lots of money. Most people cannot afford to hire lobbyists but big businesses and labor unions usually can.

They are called "lobbyists" because they tend to hang out in the lobby of the Capitol building meeting Senators and Congressmen as they pass by. Typically, a lobbyist will greet a Senator and ask for a minute to talk with him. They'll go off to the side of the lobby and the lobbyist will explain his point of view. You can visit the Capitol building where Congress meets and see lots of lobbyists talking to Senators and Congressmen. They are always using their hands to emphasize their points and usually speaking very loudly! It's fun to watch.

Why do the Senators and Congressmen take the time to talk with the lobbyists? Because many of them contribute lots of money to their political campaigns. Congressmen have to run for re-election every two years and Senators every six years. Their campaigns are very, very expensive, often costing more than ten million dollars.

To help raise that kind of money, lobbyists hold fund raisers for the Senators or Congressmen and rake in lots of cash for their campaigns. Where does the cash come from? Mainly from the people who hired the lobbyists in the first place!

Lets say that an association of all the hospitals in America did not want to see Medicaid cut. (If it were cut, their hospitals would lose a lot of money). So they hire Mr. Lobbyist to try to stop Congress from cutting Medicaid. They pay him a fee every month.

Mr. Lobbyist visits Congress and he finds out that Senator Loudmouth is the chairman of the committee that will consider the Medicaid cuts.

Senator Loudmouth has to run for re-election this year. The Senator needs money to pay for his campaign.

Mr. Lobbyist tries to persuade Senator Loudmouth to vote against cutting Medicaid. But the Senator is not persuaded. Then Mr. Lobbyist has an idea. He suggests to Senator Loudmouth that he hold a fund raiser for him to come up with money for the campaign. He says he will invite all the hospitals to send their staff to the fund raiser and give him money.

Senator Loudmouth is very happy. He will raise lots of money at the fund raiser.

Mr. Lobbyist goes back to the hospital association that hired him and says "we need to have a fund raiser for Senator Loudmouth. He is the key person who can decide whether or not to cut Medicaid."

"Why should we give him money?" the hospitals say.

"Because that way he might vote against the Medicaid cuts," Mr. Lobbyist answers.

Some people think this practice should be against the law. They say it is like paying a Senator to vote a certain way. Other people say it would be against the constitution to make that illegal. After all, they say, people have the right to tell a Senator what they think and a right to give money to his campaign. So the practice continues.

They hired lobbyists, people who are available for a fee whose job it is to try to influence the government's or Congress' decisions.

President Clinton knew that the hospitals and doctors in America hired a lot of lobbyists to help them fight against cuts in the Medicaid program. Nursing homes, where many old people lived, also hired their own lobbyists. And, finally, groups of elderly people would get together themselves and hire their own lobbyists. Everybody had a lobbyist.

And the lobbyists would spend a lot of time trying to influence the Senators and Congressmen against cutting the Medicaid program. They would get all the hospitals and doctors to donate money to the key Senators and Congressmen. This money would help to persuade Congress not to cut Medicaid.

But the Republicans wouldn't listen. They would refuse to do work with the lobbyists who supported Medicaid. They felt it was most important to cut government spending and they felt that Medicaid was one wasteful, big program. Their idea was to cut the program up into fifty pieces and give each of the fifty states control over their own program. That way the states could make the program work more efficiently and, hopefully, reduce the waste.

Republicans decided to go ahead and cut Medicaid despite what the hospitals, doctors, and lobbyists said.

But President Clinton wasn't as willing to disagree with hospitals, nurses, and their lobbyists. Most of them were Democrats and they were very important to his campaign and to the Democratic Party. Nurses, for example, tended to vote Democratic as did poor people. If they were upset with Clinton for cutting Medicaid, they might not vote for him and he could be in trouble.

So Clinton told Congress clearly: Keep the Medicaid and welfare reform issues separate. If you combine them, I will have to veto the entire bill once again.

But that suited Bob Dole just fine. He did not want a new welfare program that Bill Clinton would get credit for. He wanted to be president and he was not about to let Clinton sign a welfare bill. He would pass a bill, all right. Even a second bill now that the first one was vetoed. But it would cut Medicaid as well as welfare. And, if Clinton had to veto it, that's just too bad.

So the Republicans in the House and the Senate passed a second welfare reform bill. This time they did not cut food stamps or transportation or day care aid. They wanted to act as if they had met Clinton's objections that led him to veto the first bill. But they inserted a brand new provision cutting Medicaid.

"They know I cannot sign a bill that cuts Medicaid," Clinton complained. "What am I going to do? Throw old people out of nursing homes and ask them to live on the street? Cut off medical care to poor people? Turn them away from emergency rooms when they are in danger of dying? I can't do that."

Actually, the president was exaggerating (exaggerating means that you say something that is true but then you make it bigger or more extreme than it really is). President Clinton knew that when poor people came to hospitals seeking care and found that Medicaid wouldn't cover them, almost all doctors would treat them anyway. How would they pay for it? Most doctors and hospitals would raise their fees to other patients who could afford health insurance and use the extra money to pay for the people who got care for free. But medical costs in the US were already way too high and Clinton did not want to do anything to make them even higher.

The hospitals, doctors, nurses, poor people and their lobbyists all came to the White House to urge Clinton to veto the new welfare bill.

And the major newspapers in the country all also criticized cuts in Medicaid and demanded that Clinton veto the bill.

"If we sign the bill, we will be hurt by criticism in the Washington Post and the New York Times," said George Stephanopoulos, citing the two most important newspapers in the country. He knew – and the president knew too – that these two newspapers influenced all the others in the U.S. If they attacked the president for signing the welfare bill the Republicans passed, so would most of the other newspapers and television news shows in the U.S.

So, even though the president has a lot of power – the man with the nuclear case on his lap outside the door was a reminder of how much power he has – he always has to listen to what other people say. He has to listen to Congress or they won't pass his bills. He has to listen to the newspapers and television news channels or they will criticize him. He has to listen to lobbyists and their clients or he won't get the money for his campaign. And, most of all, he has to listen to the people or he won't get elected to another term.

But the Republicans were determined to cut Medicaid and they passed their new welfare bill with these cuts in the bill. When Clinton vetoed it again, they said, "See, he really does not want to change welfare. He was not telling the truth in the campaign. Clinton said he wanted to reform welfare but now he has twice vetoed a bill to do just that. After the first bill passed, he complained that it cut aid to day care and transportation help and food stamps but we fixed all that. We took those cuts out of the new bill, but he vetoed it anyway. You can see for yourself that he is not telling the truth about welfare. He will never sign a bill reforming welfare."

As soon as the Republican welfare bill hit President Clinton's desk, he decided to veto it again. And, in his veto statement, he repeated what he said the first time he vetoed a welfare reform bill: "I support welfare reform and if you send me a bill that accomplishes this purpose I will sign it. But I won't approve a bill that includes Medicaid cuts.

*Should we permit lobbyists to try to influence Congress?*

*Some say Yes! We cannot stop anyone from speaking to Congress whether he is paid to do so or not. We need to permit people to communicate with Congress themselves or through lawyers or lobbyists or however they want. It's a free country.*

*Others say No! The rich people can afford lobbyists and they get their way more often as a result. And a lobbyist who raises money for a Senator is really paying him a bribe and that should be illegal! (A bribe is money a person pays to a public official – like the president or a member of Congress – to get him to vote a certain way. It is a serious crime.)*

*And think about this one too:*

*Should we let the president run for a second term or should he have to leave after just one term?*

*Some say Let Him Run for Re-election! If we like him, we should be able to have him for two terms.*

*Others say No, Don't Let Him Run! If he can run for another term, he will spend his whole time in office trying to get re-elected, doing what is popular, not what is right.*

# Chapter Six:
## The People Speak Out...and The Republicans Listen

And that's where matters stood for months and months. Welfare reform seemed dead. It looked like the Republicans would never pass a bill Clinton could sign and the president would never sign a bill the Republicans would pass. Because the parties disagreed on welfare reform, it looked like it would never pass.

But wait a minute! There was one other force that wanted welfare reform to pass. It hadn't spoken out much so far, but now that it looked like the bill was dead, it began to make itself felt: The American People.

The Senators were feeling a lot of pressure from people who wanted welfare reform to pass and become law. When President Clinton had promised to reform welfare during his campaign for president, a lot of people agreed with him. It was a big reason many of them voted for him. Now they saw the president and Congress fighting over what should be in the welfare reform bill and they wanted it settled and the law passed.

Many of the Republican Senators were worried that they might not be re-elected in 1996.

The Republicans were carrying a large burden with the American people. In fact, a lot of people were pretty mad at them. Back when they took over Congress, the Republicans wanted to cut the government spending. They passed a bill to make deep cuts. President Clinton didn't agree with the cuts, so he vetoed the bill. The Republicans did not have the votes to override the veto.

So instead of accepting that they had lost, the Republicans told President Clinton: Unless you agree to the cuts we want, we will not approve any budget at all. Unless the cuts are included, we will not pass a budget.

Not pass a budget??? Nobody had ever said that.

A budget is the basic paper that lists all the money the government is allowed to spend. Under our Constitution, the government cannot spend a penny without the approval of the Congress. And when Congress does approve of the spending, they put it in the budget. But now the Republicans in Congress were saying that they would only agree on a budget that cut spending. If Clinton would not approve such a budget, then there would be no budget at all. And with no budget, there would be no permission for the

government to spend money. The government would shut down!

People wondered: "Would the Republicans really do that?" It had never happened before.

But the Republicans were quite serious and, when President Clinton refused to approve the budget cuts, the Republicans refused to pass a budget and the government had to stop spending money. All the government workers went home. The government offices all closed down. You couldn't visit national parks. A lot of airplanes couldn't fly. Tourists couldn't enter the United States. Everything just halted.

But Clinton remained very firm. He did not object to cuts in spending, he said, but he was not going to go along with the cuts in important things the Republicans wanted – like money for old people or pay for teachers. So he would not give in. And the government remained closed.

After a week or two, the Republicans were feeling too much pressure from the people in the country and they agreed to let the government re-open. Then, right around Christmas of 1995, they closed it down again and everybody got angry at them all over again. In early January of 1996,

---

## A petition?

A petition is a paper signed by lots of people asking Congress to do something. The right to sign petitions is guaranteed by the Constitution and now people were using that right to show how disturbed they were.

---

the Republicans gave in and the government opened again. Clinton had won!

But the closing and opening and closing again of the government made people very annoyed at the Republicans in Congress. They got angry and wrote letters to them and signed petitions.

Now, in the spring of 1996, Republicans were very nervous that the people who got mad at them for closing the government would not vote for them for re-election. And their stand on welfare reform was not helping them at all. People said "see, the Republicans are up to their old tricks again. First they closed the government down to cut payments to old people and now they are refusing to reform welfare and make people work for their checks unless the president agrees to cut money for old people."

So the Republican Senators went to their Majority Leader, Senator Bob Dole, and told him "we are in danger of being defeated for re-election. All of your fighting with President Clinton is hurting us and we may lose because of it."

But Dole said "I am running for president. I need to fight with Clinton because he is going to be my opponent."

"OK," the Republican Senators said, "we understand that. But don't try to run for president and be the Majority Leader of the Senate at the same time. You can't wear two hats at once!" (wearing two hats at once is a funny way of saying that you cannot do two jobs at once, particularly, if what you have to do in one job is the opposite of what you must do in the other one).

So Bob Dole had to listen to the Republican Senators and he resigned as Majority Leader in April of 1996.

# My Friendship With Trent Lott

I had known Trent for ten years. I worked in his first campaign to become a Senator and helped him to get re-elected in 1994. After he was re-elected, I visited him at his house in Gulfport, Mississippi. The home was right on the ocean – the Gulf of Mexico (which is why they called it "Gulfport"). We sat on rocking chairs and looked out at the water.

"President Clinton has called me and asked me to come back to work for him to help him to get re-elected," I told Trent.

"That's great!" he answered. "Are you going to do it?" he asked.

"Should I?" I replied.

"Darn right you should," he said. "And I have some news for you too. I am going to run for the job of Whip in the Senate." Whip is the number two job right below the Majority Leader. It has that funny name because the person who holds the job has to make sure that his Party's Senators all show up when votes are being held and to try to make sure they all vote as the Majority Leader wants them to. Because he has a hard job and sometimes needs to threaten a Senator ("If you don't vote no, I am going to make you move to a smaller office") he is called the "whip" because he uses an imaginary whip on the Senators.

"I think you will win," I told Trent.

"Me too," he answered. "And I bet Bob Dole has to resign as Leader in order to run for president. Then I will be the Majority Leader. You run the White House and I will run the Senate."

"What do we do then?" I asked.

"We pass everything!" he answered.

And guess who took his place?  My old friend Trent Lott, the Senator from Mississippi.

I called Trent after he became the new Majority Leader and said things had worked out about the way he was thinking.  I was an advisor to President Clinton and he was the boss of the Senate.  "What do we do now?" I asked.

Trent laughed and repeated what he had told me a year and a half before in Gulfport, Mississippi.  "Let's pass everything."

And that included welfare reform.

Trent realized that his Republican Senators needed to point to an accomplishment (something they had done) in the Senate to get re-elected.  If they didn't, people would say "oh, don't vote for them, all they ever do is fight, they don't actually get anything done."  No Senator wanted to hear that from his constituents right before an election. (A "constituent" is a person who lives in the district or state that the Congressman or Senator comes from.  All the constituents are allowed to vote on whether the Congressman or Senator can be re-elected so they are very powerful.

So Trent Lott called me into his office for a meeting.  But, I couldn't just walk in.  The press would be watching and everybody would wonder what we were talking about and they would write stories in their newspapers trying to figure it out.  So, here's what I had to do to see him: I called his office and said I would be right outside the building where his office was.  I used a code name.  It was "Champ" after a good friend of Trent's and mine who had just died.  So I told them "Champ is at the door outside."  Then one of Trent's staff members would hurry down to the door and bring me to his office through a back way that the press did not know about.  He called the office his "hideaway" because he could hide there and the media would never find him.  When the meeting was over, his staff would bring me back down the stairs through the secret passageway.  It was spooky and fun!

"Dick, we have to pass welfare reform," Trent told me.

"Yes, sir, we do," I answered. "President Clinton needs to accomplish something to win re-election and so do your Republican Senators. After shutting down the government, they need to do something to get well." (By get well, I did not mean that they were sick, but I meant that they needed to get well politically so they could get re-elected.)

"True," Trent agreed. "And it's good for the country," he added.

"Not just because welfare reform will work and will get people off welfare and into jobs," I replied. "But because it will show the country that the government works and can come together to get things done."

"Right," he said.

"And the funny thing is," I continued, "everything we want in a bill is in the two bills you passed. Exactly. We had to veto them because of all the other stuff you put in the bill. Just leave that stuff out and we can sign the bill."

"I know," Trent said. "A lot of folks here (in the Senate) didn't want to pass a bill the president could sign. They had other things on their mind." I knew that Trent was referring to Senator Dole, the former Majority Leader, who was running for president and did not want welfare reform to be accomplished because Dole wanted to use it as an issue in the election against President Clinton.

"But you have to take the Medicaid cuts out of the bill for Clinton to sign it," I said. "He won't sign it with those cuts in it. He won't and he can't."

"Why can't he?" Trent asked.

"Because the liberals won't let him. It's one thing to eliminate welfare unless people work. But to do that and to cut Medicaid at the same time? He can't do that. It's too much." Trent knew that I was referring to the staff people at the Health and Human Services Department who worked for Donna Shalala and the hospitals, doctors, nurses, and lobbyists who would fight against cuts in Medicaid. Shalala's people would oppose welfare reform anyway. But the doctors and hospitals wouldn't care if we changed welfare as long as we did not cut Medicaid.

"I'll see what I can do," Trent said, closing our meeting.

I reported back to President Clinton on my talk with Trent. "Sounds great," he said. He was very enthusiastic. "Now maybe they'll give me a bill I can sign."

But a few hours later, I got a phone call from George Stephanopoulos. George was very liberal and did not like welfare reform at all. He agreed with Donna Shalala that it was a bad idea and would hurt the poor. He had probably heard that I was in Lott's office – despite my attempts at keeping it secret – and was worried that I might come to an agreement with Trent Lott and the bill might pass.

"Are you negotiating with Trent on welfare reform?" he asked angrily. "We can't have everybody talking to him at once. Leon [Panetta, Clinton's chief of staff] is talking to Trent. You'll cross him up." Leon Panetta hated me because he felt that I was too conservative and worried that I would be more of an influence on the president than he was. After all, Leon just knew the president for a few years. I knew him for twenty years.

"George, I'm not freelancing here," I replied. That's Washington-speak. What I was telling him was that the president agreed that I should speak to Trent and I was keeping him closely informed about what we were discussing. "Freelancing" would have meant that I was just doing whatever popped into my head without anybody saying it was OK. But when I said I was not freelancing, I was, in effect, telling him to back off. I had the president's permission.

George got it all in an instant. "Oh" was all he said and he hung up the phone. He never bothered me about it again.

But things are never simple in Washington. At last, it seemed that welfare reform was going to pass and that the president was going to sign it.

*If a Congressman or Senator wants to vote yes on a bill and the people he represents in Congress want him to vote no, should he vote the way he thinks?*

*Some people say YES! He is put into Congress because he is a smart person who the voters want to think for him or herself and not just do whatever they want him to do.*

*Other people say NO! This is a democracy and he or she is in Congress to represent the people. He has to listen to them.*

# Chapter Seven:

## Government Workers Play a Dirty Trick on the President

But not so fast!

A thousand miles from Washington, in the state of Wisconsin, their governor, Tommy Thompson – a Republican – had gotten his legislature to pass a welfare reform of their own.

Thompson's bill was very good. It was, actually, the same bill we wanted to pass in Washington without any extra cuts and with all the good parts left in the bill. People would have to work to get benefits and there was a time limit on how long they could remain on welfare.

So now welfare reform was landing directly on President Clinton's desk in the form of the Wisconsin bill. If he approved the Wisconsin welfare plan, it would ignite a firestorm among liberals who would charge that he was eliminating help for the poor. Eliminating the safety net!

## State Power

Each of the fifty states in the US has its own state government in its own capital city. What state do you live in? What is its capital?

The Constitution says the federal government in Washington can do certain things – like impose taxes, run the army, deal with other countries and so forth. But then it says that everything else is up to the states. (Remember the tenth amendment to the Bill of Rights?) So Wisconsin could adopt its own welfare program.

But, unlike other state laws, the president needed to approve this one. That's because money from the federal government in Washington funded part of the welfare program, so the president had to approve any changes a state wanted to make.

And, if he vetoed the Wisconsin proposal, everybody would say that he wasn't really for welfare reform. After all, he would have then vetoed it twice from Congress and once when it came in from Wisconsin.

So President Clinton thought about it and decided he would approve the Wisconsin welfare bill. I was very happy. George was not.

The president called in Donna Shalala and her staff at Health and Human Services and explained to them that he had decided to approve the Wisconsin welfare bill. They moaned and groaned and criticized the bill. "It is unfair to the poor!" "It is bad for the elderly!" "It would make people starve to death!" But the president was very calm and very firm. "I am going to approve this proposal," he insisted.

The staff at Health and Human Services went crazy. They were stunned at the news. "How can we stop it?" they asked. "This is a disaster, we have to do something!" Then one of them hit on an idea!

"Let's call the New York Times (America's most important newspaper) and tell them that he has decided to veto the Wisconsin bill!" one of them suggested.

"But he just told us he is going to approve it," another staff member answered.

"I know that," the first one replied. "But don't you know that President Clinton has been criticized a lot for always changing his mind?"

"Yes, so what?"

"Well, if we tell the Times that he will veto the Wisconsin plan and he approves it instead, everybody will say that he is just changing his mind all the time and that the pressure from Republicans and conservatives was too much for him. He will look terrible. He won't do that. If we tell the newspapers that he is planning to veto the bill, he will have to do that or look very bad."

And, sure enough, the next morning the New York Times ran the headline on the front page "Clinton Waivers on Wisconsin Welfare Plan." The article said that after the president seemed to support the plan in a speech in May of 1996, he was now having doubts and that the plan could not be approved unless it was changed. Totally untrue!

It was a mean, rotten thing to do to the president. They were trying to get him to do the opposite of what he had decided. And, remember, he appointed each of them to the positions they held. They would have no power if it weren't for President Clinton and now they were trying to trap him. Sometimes politics is not nice.

But politically, the fact was that President Clinton could not change his mind in public. Too many people felt that he was always taking one position and then taking the opposite one a few weeks later. Some even said he was like a weather vane on top of your house pointing this way when the wind was blowing there and changing around when the wind changed. People said that when public opinion changed, Bill Clinton changed and that he really did not believe in anything, just in doing what would make him popular.

The accusation hurt the president very much and he was determined never to change his mind in public again. Once he took a position, he would stick with it no matter what.

But, here, he had never gotten the chance to take a position. The staff

at Health and Human Services had taken it for him and told the New York Times that he did not approve of the plan when he did.

When President Clinton saw the New York Times story, he was furious at the Health and Human Services staff. "They knew that I was going to approve the plan and they leaked the opposite to trap me into vetoing it! I want to know who did this! I want to fire that person," he threatened.

He called in the Secretary of Health and Human Services, the head of the Department, Donna Shalala. "Who told the newspapers that I was against the Wisconsin proposal? I had told everyone that I would support it!"

Donna said she had no idea who had spoken to the newspaper.

In Washington, when a government official calls a newspaper reporter and tells him something that is secret, it is called a leak – like in a boat. The reporter knows who is calling him, but he is required never to say who it was. Sometimes, the secret is "classified" which means that it is a crime to tell anyone. And there is sometimes a criminal trial but the reporter will always refuse to name the person who spoke to him. The press says that keeping their sources secret is essential to getting the news even if it breaks the law.

A lot of people disagree and it is a big fight in Washington about who is right.

But President Clinton had no way of knowing who had leaked the information. He told me he suspected that Donna Shalala herself had done it, but he couldn't prove it.

But Shalala's people had done their damage. President Clinton did not approve of the Wisconsin welfare changes. Eventually, they went into effect as part of the overall federal reform plan.

When he read the Times story about President Clinton "waivering" on the Wisconsin welfare plan, Senator Lott was very worried. He called me. "Is the president serious about welfare reform?" he asked anxiously. "Will he sign a bill if we pass it? Or will he turn against it just like he did to the Wisconsin Plan?"

Even I was worried. I called the President to ask if he still wanted me to try to get him a welfare reform bill passed. "Of course, I do," he said with anger in his voice. "I won't let these people trap me again!"

I called Trent back and told him the full story of the HHS leak to the Times and how the president had to change his mind because of it. He was amazed.

"That is the nuttiest story I have ever heard in all my years in Washington," he told me.

**Think about it...**

*Should President Clinton have approved the Wisconsin welfare reform even after the newspaper story that said he was wavering on it?*

*Some say Yes! He should stand up for principle and do what he thought was right regardless of what the staff had done.*

*Others say No! He knew that eventually it wouldn't matter if he signed a national welfare reform bill. So why get hurt politically over something that didn't matter much eventually?*

# Chapter Eight:
## Negotiating the Welfare Bill

Now, Trent had to do the hard work of persuading his fellow Republican Senators to separate the welfare reform bill from the Medicaid cuts. "You can still vote to cut Medicaid if you want but don't tie it to the welfare reform bill. If you do, Clinton will veto it," he told them.

"If we separate the two bills, he'll veto Medicaid," they answered.

"Yes," said Trent, "but he will sign welfare."

"But won't that help him get re-elected?" the Republicans asked.

"Yes," Trent conceded, "it will. He's probably going to get re-elected anyway. But you are in danger and many of our fellow Republicans are

---

## Negotiation

In a negotiation, each side starts out with what it wants and gradually, the two sides come closer together until they have a deal. Along the way, each side figures out how strongly the other feels about each issue. For example, it was pretty clear that the Republicans were more worried about the amount of money spent on transportation and day care and a bit less opposed to the money for food stamps. So we let them cut where they wanted to but got more in food stamps than we originally thought.

Why would the Republicans feel willing to spend money on food stamps? Because many of them came from farming states like Nebraska and Kansas. The more the government spent on food stamps, the more the farmers in those states would earn. So they were willing to see food stamps rise.

In Washington, Senators and Congressmen usually believe in certain general principles. Republicans want to cut spending and Democrats want to add more spending. But, for example, when the question is money for farmers, Republicans who come from farm states forget about their overall opinions and press for more money for farmers just like the Democrats do. Ideas are important. But getting the votes of the people of your home state or district are always more important to Congressmen and Senators.

---

in danger of defeat. If they lose, we would lose control over the Senate. Think first of yourself and your fellow Senators. Passing this bill will help us all get re-elected. And, its good for the country. We need welfare reform. Lets stop playing games and get it passed."

Trent did his magic. He proudly called me in early July of 1996 and said that he had persuaded the Republicans to separate the two bills. "You will get a bill without Medicaid in it," he promised.

Clinton was very happy, but still a little suspicious of the Republicans. "I wonder what else they will put in the bill to try to get me to veto it?"

I checked with Trent and, sure enough, a lot of the cuts from the first bill were back in this bill. Cuts in food stamps, transportation, day care, and so forth. The bill even cut funds for diapers for children. We began a four way discussion. Trent would tell me what the Republicans wanted. I would tell the president. Clinton would tell me what he could accept, I would tell Trent and he would tell the other Republicans. This kind of discussion goes on all the time in Washington. It is called a "negotiation."

Things were going pretty well in our discussions with Trent Lott, when a new issue came up. Some Republicans said they did not want welfare benefits to go to people who were not American citizens.

Not all the people who live in the United States are citizens. About one person out of every ten that lives here is not a citizen. To be a citizen means that you are loyal to your country. You can live anywhere you want, but you can generally be a citizen of only one country. If you are a citizen of France, for example, but live in the United States, your first loyalty is to France. You can be called up to serve in the army in France if there is a war. You get the right to vote in France (but not in the United States).

Everybody agreed that illegal immigrants should not get welfare benefits. But the question was: Should people who come here legally, live here and pay their taxes be able to get welfare and other government benefits even though they are not citizens?

The Republicans wanted to stop them from getting any government benefits. This would not only apply to welfare but to other important

# Citizenship

The Constitution says that to become a citizen, you either have to be born in the United States or go through a process to become a citizen called "naturalization." To become a naturalized citizen, you have to pass a test showing you know something about our history and government and you have to take an oath, before God, swearing your loyalty to the United States.

Many people who live in the United States do not want to become citizens. They want to remain citizens of the countries they came from. They just live here because their jobs are here or their family is here.

Of the people who live here but are not citizens, some are here legally and others are not. To live in the United States legally – so you are not breaking the law by living here – you need to get a "visa" from the government. A visa says its OK to come into the United States and stay here. Some visas are for one year. Some are for longer periods. When your visa time is over, you have to leave.

But some people don't want to leave and others come in even though they have never had any visa at all. About half of the people who are not citizens and who live here anyway are in this group. They live here even though it is breaking the law. Our government doesn't like it when people live here illegally. Many of them are arrested and sent home each year. That is called a "deportation."

But most of the people who live here illegally do not get deported and just continue to live and work here.

programs as well. For example, the government pays everyone who is disabled to make up for their loss of income. If you are hurt in a car accident and cannot do your job anymore because of your injury, the government will make up part of your lost pay.

The Republicans wanted to cut off disability payments to anyone who was not a citizen. They said that if you don't want to accept the responsibilities of citizenship you shouldn't benefit from the government programs.

President Clinton didn't see it that way. "Take a guy who is here legally but is not a citizen. He works every day and pays his taxes which includes his taxes for Social Security and for disability insurance. If he is hurt crossing the street, the Republicans do not want to give him disability benefits. But he paid the tax, so why can't he get the benefit?"

But the larger question was why were the Republicans adding all this stuff to the welfare reform bill? A lot of the president's friends believed that the Republicans were playing a game, constantly passing welfare reform bills and then always adding something at the last minute that had nothing to do with welfare reform that would force the president to veto the bill. The president's wife, First Lady Hillary Clinton shared these doubts. "They just want to make Bill veto the bill over and over again. They are playing us for fools," she warned.

I complained to Trent. I said "the president thinks you are always adding new provisions that we cannot live with to each welfare bill you pass."

But Trent came right back at me. "You are the ones who are moving the goalposts." (It's a football phrase. You go to the goal line and think you have scored a touchdown but the other team picks up the goal posts and moves them ten yards back and says, "no, you still have ten yards to go to score a touchdown.") He explained, "First you said we had to include money for transportation and day care and food stamps in the bill. We did that. Then you said we had to take Medicaid out of the bill. We did that

too. And now you are saying that we cannot limit benefits for non-citizens. Each time you are making it harder and harder to pass the bill.

Each side had a good point. Seeing the situation from their own point of view, it did look like the other side was adding more and more demands. And, because the president and the Republicans did not trust each other and the election was only a few months away, they each had doubts that the other side really wanted to reach a deal and pass a welfare reform bill.

So Senator Lott and the president agreed on some things. They agreed that the bill had to give money for transportation, day care, food stamps, and diapers. They agreed that people on welfare who took jobs should get money from the government so that it paid for them to work (that they

## A compromise?

Compromise means that two sides disagreed but that they each accepted only part of what they wanted and agreed on a deal. For example, lets say I want you to pay me 50 cents for a glass of Lemonade. But you only want to pay 25 cents. We argue about it for a few minutes. Then we come to a compromise. You pay 25 cents but I will only give you half a glass of Lemonade. We each got part of what we wanted but not the whole thing.

made more money working than they would if they got welfare benefits and did not work).

But they also disagreed on one very important thing: Senator Lott, Speaker Gingrich, and the Republicans in Congress insisted that legal immigrants not get welfare or any other form of government benefits. And President Clinton insisted that they should get them.

On this issue, there was to be no compromise.

**Think about it...**

*Is it right for people who are not citizens but are here legally to get welfare?*

*Some say YES! They are our guests who came to this country legally. They pay taxes while they are here. If they fall on hard times and need our help to get by, we should give it to them.*

*Some say NO! They can stay here or leave. If they are not doing well here, go home. A lot of other countries do not pay any welfare benefits to poor people or pay less benefits than we do. If we pay welfare to people who are not citizens, lots of people will come here just to go on welfare.*

# Chapter Nine:
## Will President Clinton Sign or Veto the Welfare Reform Bill???

President Clinton's advisers and staff in the White House were split on whether or not the president should agree to sign a welfare reform bill. I urged Clinton to sign it. But most of the others on the White House staff wanted him to veto it. George Stephanopoulos and Chief of Staff Leon Panetta were especially strong in opposing the bill.

George urged the president to veto it for political reasons. "You will lose support among blacks (African-Americans) and Hispanics. They won't go to the polls to vote for you on election day. The liberals will attack you if you sign the bill. They will say that you are condemning millions of people to deeper poverty."

And the labor unions, a key part of the Democratic Party, also opposed the bill. Labor unions are organizations of workers in a business who

## The Right To Demonstrate

Our Constitution gives everyone the right to hold public demonstrations – as long as they are peaceful – to express their ideas and tell the president and Congress what they think. They are allowed to picket outside the White House. "Picketing" is when they carry signs saying what they believe and march back and forth in front of the White House. Often they sing songs and chant slogans to press their ideas.

get together to fight for better wages and other changes that will make their lives better. The unions did not like the idea that the welfare reform bill gave welfare mothers jobs that could go to union members instead.

For example, if the government gave a welfare mother a job sweeping up schools after the children had gone home, what about the janitor whose job it was to sweep up the school? Wouldn't the welfare mother be taking away his job? And since the government was paying the welfare mother benefits anyway, she was working for free.

The unions called the welfare reform bill the "Slave Labor Bill" because it forced welfare mothers to work and paid them nothing extra for their work, nothing more than they would anyway from welfare.

The labor unions are very powerful in the Democratic Party. They give lots of money to Democratic candidates – including President Clinton. And their members work hard at getting other union members out to vote on election day to help elect Democratic candidates. No Democratic president wanted to do anything to make the labor unions angry.

Donna Shalala and the Health and Human Services Department, of course, were especially strong in urging the president to veto the welfare reform bill. They had opposed it twice before and had opposed the Wisconsin Plan. Now they sensed that the most important battle had come and they were determined to stop the bill from becoming law.

They called poor people and their political organizations all over the country to protest and demonstrate to urge the president to veto the bill.

"Don't force us to leave our children," one of the signs said. By that, they meant that the bill would make welfare mothers work and they would have to leave their children during the day. People who supported welfare reform pointed out that everybody who works has the same problem and if we all stayed home with our children all the time, who would get the money to feed our families?

Other signs said "Don't throw us out on the street." That slogan meant that the time limits on welfare would cut off benefits after five years whether or not the person had a job. "Suppose a person could not get a job," they argued, "isn't it unfair to cut off all their benefits?"

One of the strongest voices against signing the bill came from the president's wife, the First Lady Hillary Clinton. She asked to meet with me to talk about it. "You know that Bill and I support welfare reform and always have," she told me. "But I am very concerned about the bill that the Republicans have passed. It not only cuts welfare, it also denies any benefits to people who are legally here in America but who are not citizens. That's unfair."

I pointed out to Hillary that I was the president's political advisor. "My job is to help him get re-elected." Hillary had pushed the president very strongly to call me after he lost the House in 1994 and was always a strong supporter of my efforts. I told her that I did not think the president could be re-elected if he vetoed the welfare reform bill. "After making so much noise about welfare reform, to veto three bills looks like he was not sincere when he said he favored welfare reform."

And then I told Hillary something else. "You and I have worked together for a long time," I reminded her. (We had worked together for twenty years.) I continued, "If the president signs the welfare reform bill, he will get re-elected and will probably get control of Congress again. After that, he can change the welfare reform bill so it is more to his liking. But right now, your choice is to take it or leave it – sign the bill as Congress passed it or veto it – and I do not feel your husband will get re-elected if he vetoes the bill."

Hillary smiled at me and said, "You silver tongued devil, you." By that she meant that she saw my point of view and was OK with her husband signing the bill.

But every part of the Democratic Party came down against the bill and made it very hard for the president to sign it.

The issue came to a climax at the end of July of 1996. On July 31, 1996, the House of Representatives passed the welfare reform bill by a vote of 328-100. That seemed like a big margin, but the Democrats in the House, split right in half on it. 98 Democrats voted yes and 97 voted no. The situation in the Senate was the same. On August 1, 1996, the Senate passed the bill by 88-21. Again, the Democrats were split with 25 voting yes and 21 voting no.

So the president faced a deeply divided Democratic Party as the bill appeared on his desk.

President Clinton did not tell anyone (including me) whether he would sign or veto the welfare reform bill. Everybody wondered and every single day all the newspapers and television programs were filled with political experts guessing about what he would do.

That August, both of the parties were scheduled to hold their national conventions to nominate their candidates for president.

# National Conventions

Each party has a convention every four years to nominate their candidate for president. While the people elect the president, each political party chooses its own candidate for president - the person they want the voters to elect. This person is called the "nominee" because he

has been chosen (nominated) by his party. He then has to face the nominee of the other party and the voters choose between then.

The conventions weren't just where the party's nominee was chosen. In fact, from that point of view, they didn't matter much at all. By the time they met, everybody knew who the party would nominate. Back fifty years ago, people did not know who the convention would nominate until it did so. That was because both political parties let the leaders of the party choose who the nominee would be. These party leaders were often called "political bosses" and they would decide who would represent the party at the next election. Back then, the convention was very important and everybody listened closely on radio (television and the Internet were not yet invented) to find out who won the nomination.

But then in 1968, the Democratic Party nominated a man most people in the party did not want to be president (his name was Hubert Humphrey). At the time, the United States was fighting a war in Vietnam (vee-et-nam) and thousands of young men were dying. Most Americans wanted the war to end, but Humphrey wanted it to continue. When the bosses nominated Humphrey even though he was for the war, the voters who would normally vote Democrat refused to do so. And the Republican, Richard Nixon, won.

The Democratic Party was very upset by the results of the 1968 election and sat down and changed the way they decided who would be the party's candidate. No longer would they let bosses make the decision. Now the voters who backed the Democratic Party would vote in their own elections – called primaries – to decide who it would be. As a result, the conventions lost a lot of their real role since everyone knew that the winner of the primaries would be the party's candidate. Soon after, the Republican Party followed the lead of the Democrats and changed their rules too so primaries determined the nominee of the party. The political bosses were dead.

But the conventions were still important because they were covered by television and each night – the conventions last four nights – the leaders of the party give speeches. It sounds boring, but it's not. Everybody wonders what they will say and whether the impression the party leaves on the voters who are watching will be good or bad. Everyone is especially interested in the last night of the convention when the candidate for president gives his major speech, explaining what he wants to do if he is elected president. Almost everyone in the country watches those speeches, even now.

President Clinton said that he would wait until after the Republican Party convention was over so that he could better understand what he was up against in the election coming up that November.

The polls showed that Bill Clinton was way ahead of Bob Dole as the Republican convention opened. Some polls had him as much as 17 points ahead.

## Polling

A poll is another word for a public opinion survey. The idea behind the survey or the poll is pretty simple but very hard to believe. It says that if you ask five hundred or one thousand people what they think about an important question, then their answers will be the same percentage yes and percentage no as you would get if you asked every person in the entire country! In other words, the 500 or 1,000 people you ask will have the exact same opinion as all 310,000,000 (three hundred and ten million) people who live in the United States!

Of course, you can't just ask any thousand people. If you asked everybody in your family or who lived on your street or in your town, you would not find out what people who lived in other places felt and thought.

So the idea is that you ask a certain number of people in each of the fifty states and in each part of each state depending on what the total number of people living there is. For example, Dallas, Texas has about two million people who live there out of 310 million who live in America. That means that about six out of every one thousand people in America live in Dallas. So you find six people in Dallas and ask them what they think and you do the same in each part of the country.

Polling companies take surveys all the time and they are almost always accurate and tell us what the entire country is thinking.

As the Republican Convention approached, the polls showed that President Clinton was far ahead of the likely Republican candidate Bob Dole. But that was before the Republican convention was held. After it, who knew what the situation would be?

The Republicans held their convention that year in San Diego, California. Each year each party chooses a different city in which to hold their convention. And the Republican Convention was very, very good. It persuaded a lot of people to vote for them and against President Clinton.

The highlight came on Wednesday night – the third night of the four night convention – when Bob Dole's wife, Elizabeth Dole, spoke to the country.

Elizabeth was pretty well known even before she married Bob. And that night, she gave the best speech she had ever given.

A lot of people respected Bob Dole. He was a soldier in World War II and was wounded very badly. He almost died. And even now, he cannot use his right arm, only his left one. In politics, he was always fighting against government spending, against abortion, and for morality and family values.

People respected Dole but they didn't really know him and sometimes didn't really like him.

So Elizabeth devoted her speech to telling people what Bob was really like. She had a great way to do it. She didn't just stand up there and say good things about her husband. After all, many wives can do that. Instead she had brought with her into the Convention a lot of people who knew Bob Dole during his life and she went out on the floor of the Convention with a microphone in her hand and asked each of them to tell a story about Bob.

The men who served with him in the Army were there. The nurse and doctor who helped him recover from his wounds were there. Some people who were disabled (like Bob Dole) and could not get government help were there to explain how Bob helped them get the aid they needed. Elizabeth told how one Thanksgiving, Bob invited 35 young people from "tough parts" of Washington, D.C. where they lived to come to dinner and tell about their lives. People from Kansas, Bob's home state, were in the audience and they talked about how he helped them get government benefits or jobs. It was pretty impressive.

Bob Dole himself spoke the next night – on the fourth night of the convention. Everybody was really interested in what he would say because

they had learned so many good things about him from Elizabeth's speech. And guess what Bob Dole said?  He said that Bill Clinton had twice vetoed welfare reform and was not going to change welfare at all.  He said that when Bill Clinton told everybody he was a moderate, he was not telling the truth – that he was still very much a liberal.  He said that Clinton becoming more of a moderate was just something he said, not something he really meant.

That put Clinton on the spot.  The Congress had passed the welfare reform bill and he would have to decide whether or not to sign it.  After Dole's speech, there would be a lot of pressure for him to sign it.

The polls showed that the Republican Convention had really succeeded in helping Dole.  Before the Convention, the polls had said that Clinton was 17 points ahead.  But now, after just four days of the Convention, Dole was only 7 points behind Clinton.

That meant that his election could depend on what he did about welfare reform.

About half of the Democrats did not want Clinton to sign the bill. The pickets outside the White House all wanted him to veto the bill. Labor unions and Clinton's staff at the White House and a lot of the lobbyists wanted him to veto the bill.

But the other half of the Democratic Party wanted him to sign the welfare bill. They believed in welfare reform and thought it was a good idea to make people work in order to get benefits. They wanted people to have only a certain amount of time on welfare and then to have to leave and support themselves.

The Republicans were very happy. They figured they would win either way. If Clinton signed the welfare bill, he would make half of his party very angry at him and they might not back him in the coming election. And if Clinton vetoed the bill, the Republicans could tell the country that he had not told them the truth when he said in his first campaign that he wanted to "end welfare as we know it" and that he was really not a moderate but a liberal after all.

The Republicans wanted to embarrass Clinton before the Democratic Convention. So they passed the bill at the end of July and on the first day of August, knowing that it meant that President Clinton would have to sign or veto the bill in the three weeks between the Republican Convention, in early August and the Democratic Convention which started on August 26th. That way Clinton would have to make his decision before his own convention met.

Republicans were hoping that the people who were mad at the president's decision would refuse to support him and would say so at the Democratic Convention. The Democrats would be split, just like they were over the Vietnam War in 1968 and the Republicans hoped that, like then, they would win as a result.

Everybody looked to President Bill Clinton and asked one single question: Are you going to sign or veto this bill? It had become not only the most important question in the country, but one of the most important decisions a president has ever had to make.

And none of us knew what Clinton was going to do.

The president spent many days after the Congress passed the bill asking people for their advice. And the people he asked were also split. Some said "sign." Others said "veto."

The president called me the night he was making the decision. "I want to sign the bill," he began. "I strongly believe that we should make people on welfare work. I think that it would help get them started on lives of working and wouldn't let them stay dependent on checks from the government every week."

But the president was very angry about the cuts in payments to immigrants. It was OK with him to limit welfare so it would not go to those who have come here illegally. "They broke the law when they came here without asking for our permission so we should not give them welfare benefits," he said. "But those who came here under our laws surely deserve our protection."

"If you veto the bill over that," I said, "nobody will believe that you did it out of concern for legal immigrants. After all, they can always go home if they don't like our system and, anyway, they cannot vote here." I warned that "this will be the third time you have vetoed a welfare reform bill. It will persuade everyone that Bob Dole is right that you do not want to sign a bill like that no matter how it is presented to you."

That made the president angry. He shouted into the telephone. I could imagine how his face turned red when he was upset and how the veins stood out on his neck. It was not a pretty sight. "I have been begging for a welfare reform bill," he said with his voice filled with emotion. "I have been pleading for a welfare reform bill. I have negotiated in good faith

## What Is Asylum?

Some people come to the United States because they are not free in their own countries to say and write what they think. They cannot criticize their government or their president like we can here. If they get into trouble in their own country for speaking out, they can ask the United States to let them come here to avoid having to go to jail. That is called applying for "asylum." The president was saying that these people were not free to go back to their own countries. They would be put in prison.

for a welfare reform bill. Why won't they send me a welfare reform bill without any other provisions?" His voice became very loud at the end.

"Calm down," I said. "The Republicans want to make you cut aid to immigrants. They have wanted it for a very long time."

"So why don't they just pass a bill to do it? Why put it in the welfare reform bill?" he demanded.

"Because you'd veto it," I answered. "The only way they can get you to sign a bill for these cuts for aid to immigrants is if they put it in a welfare reform bill."

I pressed the issue with the president. "Why are you so concerned with aid to immigrants? They cannot vote in our elections and they can always go home or to another country if they are unhappy with the law here."

"Many of them can't go home," he said. "Some are here because they asked for asylum (a-sigh-lum)."

"And," the president continued, "what if a person is here legally and is hit by a truck crossing the street? Suppose he is laid up in the hospital and cannot walk? Suppose he needs rehabilitation and special treatment so he can walk again? Under this new law, we would not pay him disability benefits. He couldn't leave. He can't walk. But he cannot afford to get help here."

"But he is not a citizen," I answered.

"I know he's not," the president replied. "But he is here legally and every single week he pays for disability insurance out of his paycheck just like a citizen does. Then when he needs to collect on his insurance, all of a sudden, we won't cover it. That's not fair."

I had to agree with the president. But I repeated to him that I felt that he had to sign the bill even with that bad provision in it.

"If you sign the bill," I said, "I have no doubt that you will be re-elected this year. And by a pretty good margin. That should be enough for you to bring in a Democratic Senate and House. Then you can pass whatever changes you need in the bill."

(Usually, when a president from one political party won a national election or re-election, it encouraged people to vote for the members of his party for Senate and for Congress. I was saying that enough of them would do so in order for the Democrats to take over the Senate and the House which they had just lost two years before).

"You think so?" the president asked.

I wasn't so sure, so I shifted my argument. "And, even if you don't get control, the governors of the states will never approve of cutting off disability benefits for legal immigrants."

"Why not?" he asked, curious.

"Because if there is no federal aid available, they will end up having to

### Bill Signing

When a president signs a particularly important bill, he has a ceremony – an event attended by the media and by the Senators and Congressmen who supported the bill. He sometimes even signs the bill using a different pen for each letter of his name and hands the pens to these people as a souvenir of the bill signing and as a way of thanking them for their help in passing it. At the ceremony, he makes a short speech. I was suggesting that the president tell people in his speech about the changes he wanted to make in the bill.

pay the costs of people who enter their hospitals without federal aid to pay for them."

I knew I was right on this argument. Hospitals in the United States really almost never turn away patients who are in real need of care. If a person is dying or has been badly hurt in an accident, he will go to an emergency room of his local hospital and will get treatment. If he cannot pay for it himself, or there is no government aid to pay for it, the hospital will provide the care for free. But the doctors and the nurses still must be paid and the medicines that they use in treating him still cost money. So who pays? Sometimes, as we have discussed earlier in this book, the hospital charges other patients more, but usually the state government usually has to give the hospital money to be sure it stays open and pays its bills. The governors of the fifty states would not want to have to pay for these cases if benefits to legal immigrants were cut off.

"So you think I can sign this bill and, at the same time, suggest the ways in which it should be amended?" Clinton asked.

"Exactly, use the signing ceremony to criticize the very bill you are signing and ask the Congress to take it up again next year. You can even say that if you are re-elected, changing the bill will be important to you. You can shout it from the rooftops as you are signing the bill."

"That might be the answer," the president said as he thought about my idea. "I could appeal to the governors to press Congress to change the bill next year and even organize the effort myself."

I could hear what the president was saying. But sometimes it is more important to hear what he was not saying but was thinking. I believe he was saying to himself that if he criticized the bill as he was signing it and promised to change it next year, that the people who would be angry with him for cutting benefits to immigrants would not be as upset and would still support him.

And, so it was that President Clinton decided to sign the welfare reform bill.

*Do you think President Clinton should have signed the welfare reform bill?*

*Some say Yes! It was very important to make welfare mothers work and to limit the time on welfare. The fact that the President did not like some of the other things in the bill is beside the point. Nothing is perfect. And the president could not let this historic chance slip away.*

*Others say No! He should not have signed a bill he did not agree with. If he thought the cuts in aid to legal immigrants were wrong, he should have refused to sign the bill at all.*

# Chapter Ten:
## How Did He Sign the Bill?

When the president started to tell his top staff that he was going to sign the bill, they were shocked. Almost all of them had wanted him to veto it. I was about the only one who wanted him to approve it. So, naturally, I was very happy.

But now that the president agreed to sign it, the first question now was: When should he sign it? The Constitution gives the president ten days to sign the bill. The Republicans had just passed the bill and were hoping to make the president sign or veto right before his own party's convention. They knew that the welfare reform bill passed with half of the Democratic Congressmen voting yes and the other half voting no. They were hoping that those who opposed the bill would be upset if the president signed it and might even refuse to attend the Democratic Convention in protest.

### Ten Days To Sign A Bill

The Constitution says the president has to act within ten days. But that is ten days after the bill reaches his desk. In this case, the Republicans did not want the president to sign the bill before their own national convention. That would have looked bad for them and would have made it impossible for them to attack the president over welfare reform. (Bob Dole would have had to rewrite his speech!)

So the Congress did not send the bill over to the president until August 13, giving the president until August 23 to sign the bill. The president signed it on August 22nd.

The president motioned for George Stephanopoulos and me to

come into the Oval Office (the West Wing official office of the president). He had a worried expression on his face. "How can I sign this bill?" he asked us.

I said it was simple, just "sign your name at the bottom."

The president was annoyed and turned to Stephanopoulos and said "George, how do I do it?"

Of course, he was referring to the bad experience he had with the Wisconsin welfare plan where he told his staff and the people at Donna Shalala's Department of Health and Human Services that he was going to sign the Wisconsin plan and then they told the newspapers that he was "wavering" on it. He did not want to be caught in a trap like that again.

George, who is skilled in the way Washington works, thought about it for a while and told the president his idea. Clinton nodded his head and we set the plan in motion.

We had decided that he would sign the bill right before the Democratic Convention started. And we would follow George's script to the letter.

That morning, the president did not tell anyone that he was planning to sign the welfare reform bill that day. He felt that he couldn't because the opponents of the bill might leak the wrong information to the press just like they had when he let them in on his confidence and told them he was going to approve the Wisconsin bill. So, instead of saying what he was going to do, he acted as if he had not made up his mind and called a meeting to advise him on whether or not to sign it. He held the meeting in the building next to the White House where most of the staff have their offices, called the Old Executive Office Building.

### The Old Executive Office Building

More than five hundred people work on the White House staff. The White House building itself is pretty small and only about fifty of them can fit their offices in it. The others work next door in a bigger building called the "Old Executive Office Building." It was there that the president set up the meeting.

It is much fancier than the White House. Originally, it was the home of the State Department where a lot of foreign leaders came to meet with the Secretary of State. Some of the rooms have painted ceilings with clouds and blue sky painted on the plaster.

But, because the president only had ten days to decide, the Republicans had fixed it so that he had no choice but to sign it right before his Convention met.

The president set the meeting for 10:00 AM and asked everyone to be sure to be on time. He invited all the people who had been with him when he discussed whether or not to sign the Wisconsin plan and a few others. He had the Vice-President Al Gore and the White House Chief of Staff Leon Panetta with him. He, Gore and Panetta sat at a long table in the front of the room (called a dais) while the others sat in chairs facing them.

One by one, the president called on each of the people in the meeting to come to the front of the room and explain whether they thought he should sign or veto the welfare reform bill and tell him why they thought that way. All of the staff people there wanted him to veto the bill and they were very eager to tell him why. They went on and on and on. It seemed to take forever.

But President Clinton – who had already decided to sign the bill – did not get bored. He sat there while they all talked on, asking them good questions. As they spoke, he wrote notes of what they were saying.

Finally, at about 11:45, almost two hours after the start of the meeting, the president stood up and said "this meeting is wonderful. I am getting so many good ideas about welfare from it. I am learning things I never heard before. I want the meeting to continue. Don't break for lunch. I'd like you all to stay here. I have to go to the White House to meet a foreign leader who is there to see me. I will see him for about fifteen minutes and then I will come right back. In the meantime, Al (Gore) and Leon (Panetta) will stay here and tell me what you have said while I was away. But please continue, I will be right back.

Then, still following George's script, he slipped out the door and went to the White House, just a short walk away. Before he had left, the president had secretly ordered a table set up in the Rose Garden (right outside his Oval Office door) and had the press come at noon. As soon as the press was there, President Clinton signed the welfare reform bill. All the time, the staff people in the Old Executive Office Building were talking on and on about how he should veto it. They did not know that even as they were speaking, he was signing the bill right next door!

As the president said he would, when he signed the bill, he criticized the cuts in aid to immigrants and called for it to be changed the next year. (And

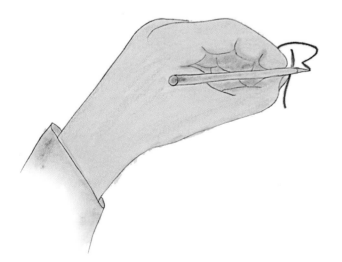

it was. Clinton's Democrats did not win Congress in the elections of 1996 although the president was re-elected. But the nation's governors pressed Congress to fix the law so that they did not have to pay for the health care of legal immigrants. The governors were

mainly Republicans so the Republican leaders in Congress had to listen to them. Gingrich and Lott both admitted that they had been wrong to cut off the aid in the first place and eliminated the cuts, just as President Clinton had wanted all along).

The staff from the Health and Human Services Department were very angry when they left the meeting to find out the welfare reform bill was now signed and already the law of the land. Two even quit their jobs in protest. But since they had misbehaved when the president told them about the Wisconsin bill, they just could not be trusted a second time.

The whole country – or most of it – exploded in celebration when they got the news that the bill had been signed and was finally the law of the land! The newspapers ran large headlines announcing that President Clinton had signed the bill. Many said it was a new day in how the government treated the poor. But those who opposed it still thought it was a mistake for the president to sign the bill. And the Republicans felt badly because they could not use the issue against the president in the election.

But the fact is that the welfare reform bill worked even better than anybody had ever expected. Looking back, almost everyone agrees that it was a very good idea.

When the president signed the bill, there were 12 million people on welfare. Ten years later, there were only 5 million. Six out of ten of the mothers who left welfare got jobs.

And the number of children from poor families dropped by more than ten million.

On the tenth anniversary of the welfare reform bill, President Clinton, himself, said, "The 1996 Welfare Act shows us how much we can achieve when both parties bring their best ideas to the negotiating table and focus on doing what is best for the country."

He stressed that "neither side got exactly what it had hoped for." But he said that "we compromised to reach an agreement, but we never betrayed our principles and we passed a bill that worked."

It's easy to see why the number of people on welfare dropped now that they had to work to get benefits, but why did the number of poor children drop also?

It dropped because millions of mothers who had been living on very small incomes that came from welfare checks, left those behind and took jobs that paid well. And they got all the extra benefits that President Clinton had insisted on: day care, transportation, food stamps and, most importantly, an extra check from the government that paid them *to* work just as welfare had paid them *not* to work.

Part of the reason for the success was an idea that President Clinton made sure was in the bill he signed. His idea was instead of giving money to people for not working, why not give money to companies who hire them to work? He realized that it cost money for a company to hire someone who was on welfare. Chances are that they did not have a lot of work experience, training, or degrees from high school or college. The company that was hiring them would have to spend a lot of its own money training them to do the job properly. Some even had to teach them to read and write, because the schools may not have done that when they were young.

So President Clinton included a program in the bill that gave every company that hired a person off the welfare rolls $7,000 (seven thousand dollars) during their first year of work and then, if they stayed on the job, $10,000 (ten thousand dollars) for the second year. The law gave the companies the money in the form of a tax credit. That meant that the company could keep the money itself. So if a company owed the government $50,000 in taxes and they hired a worker off welfare, they would only owe the government $43,000 the first year and $40,000 the second year.

So it made sense for companies to hire people who were on welfare since the government was going to pay part of the cost. But would they keep paying the workers after the second year? Nobody knew. But when the third year came around, almost all the companies continued to keep the people who had been on welfare on the payroll. They were skilled then and were doing good jobs. Most of them still have their jobs even today or have moved on to better jobs in other companies.

President Clinton worked very hard after he signed the welfare reform bill to get companies to hire people who had been on welfare. He formed an organization of big companies who agreed to hire thousands of people who were on welfare and announced it to the press. Sometimes he would invite the heads of the companies to come to the White House for a big dinner or luncheon honoring them for helping out. So most of the very large companies hired people off of welfare and the program became one of America's biggest successes.

Both Presidents Bush and Obama continued President Clinton's welfare reform program and it has been one of the best in history.

# Chapter Eleven:
## Conclusion

I sn't it funny how our government works?  The Democrats and Republicans always fight with each other.  That's what they are supposed to do.  Each wants to defeat the other one.  When a president talks to the members of the other party, he knows that everyone he is talking to is going to vote against him and do everything he can to defeat him.

And yet, it works for one reason:  The two parties are both eager to win support from the people.  The people listen closely to their arguments with each other.  Sometimes they side with the Democrats.  Sometimes they side with the Republicans.  (Even some Democrats often side with the Republicans and even some Republicans often side with the Democrats!)

As the debate goes on, the people make up their minds.

Then a time comes when the people say "OK, I've heard enough. I have reached a conclusion."

Very rarely is the conclusion entirely for one party or the other. Usually they feel that both parties are a little right and a little wrong. But they go through the issues and decide who is right on each question.

Look at welfare reform and consider each of the separate questions that came before the Congress and the people and how the people decided:

1. Republicans said welfare mothers should have to work. Most Democrats said no. People sided with the Republicans. They should all work.

2. Republicans said we are spending too much money on daycare for the children of welfare mothers. Democrats said we need to spend the money so they can leave home and work. People decided Democrats were right about this one.

3. Republicans said we should cut the amount of money for transportation for welfare mothers. Democrats said we needed to spend the money so they could get to work. Now, again, people felt the Democrats were right.

4. Democrats said it was wrong to kick someone off welfare after five years. Republicans said it was the right thing to do. People agreed with the Republicans.

And so on. Each question was argued in public and the people came to a conclusion.

And once they made a decision, the politicians of both parties had to follow it. If they did not, they would not be re-elected. So our system works. We argue like crazy. But once the people decide, we go ahead and do what they want.

And that is why America is a great country!

# Author Biography

Dick worked for President Bill Clinton in the White House from 1994 until 1996. He was in charge of President Clinton's re-election and was very involved in passing the welfare reform legislation.

He had also been the consultant to the chief Republican, Senate Majority Leader Trent Lott when he was elected to the Senate, so he worked with them both to pass the welfare bill.

He has been on FoxNews for fifteen years and now has a radio show in Philadelphia on Newstalk 1210 WPHT.

He and his wife, Eileen McGann, have written sixteen books and three more for children. The children's books tell about their dog Dubs as he travels to Washington and Philadelphia to see the greatness of America and as he runs for president.

They live in Florida.

. . . . . . . . . . . . . . . . . . . . . . . .

Clayton J. Liotta is an artist, illustrator, and cartoonist. His cartoon series, The Wood Road, can be found on Facebook and you can also visit him at liottastudios.com.